WHAT'S THE SCORE?

Sports Jokes
Compiled by Charles Keller
Illustrated by Stan Mack

Prentice-Hall, Inc. / Englewood Cliffs, New Jersey

Printed in the United States of America   ·J
Prentice-Hall International, Inc., London
Prentice-Hall of Australia, Pty. Ltd., North Sydney
Prentice-Hall of Canada, Ltd., Toronto
Prentice-Hall of India Private Ltd., New Delhi
Prentice-Hall of Japan, Inc., Tokyo
Prentice-Hall of Southeast Asia Pte. Ltd., Singapore
Whitehall Books Limited, Wellington, New Zealand

10   9   8   7   6   5   4   3   2   1

Library of Congress Cataloging in Publication Data
Keller, Charles.   What's the score?
Summary: Compilation of jokes for children
about sports.
1. Sports—Anecdotes, facetiae, satire, etc.
2. Wit and humor, Juvenile. [1. Sports—
Anecdotes, facetiae, satire, etc. 2. Jokes]
I. Mack, Stanley, ill.   II. Title.
PN6231.S65K44   818'.5402   81-10575
ISBN 0-13-955021-6   AACR2

For Betsy, Carol, Marjie, and Ronnie

Don't you know that fishing isn't allowed here?
I'm not fishing. I'm teaching my worm to swim.

My doctor told me I can't play tennis.
Oh, he's played with you, too.

Boy, that football player can really fly down the field.
Naturally, he's a wingback.

Which Olympic hockey team skates the fastest?
The USSR, because they are always Russian.

What was the score in the football game against the
   Mummies?
It was all tied up.

What do gymnasts and bananas have in common?
They both can do splits.

The pitcher on our baseball team is not so good.
What do you mean?
He has four basic pitches—a fast ball, a slow ball, a
   curve, and one that reaches the plate.

Why did the baseball player marry the baker?
To make a better batter.

What is the score of the game?
Ten to seven.
Who's winning?
Ten.

Why did the long-distance runner go to the
   veterinarian?
Because his calves hurt.

I hear you've been taking a mail-order body-building course.

That's right. Each week my mailman brings me a new piece of equipment.

You don't look any different to me.

No, but you should see my mailman.

Why would a spider make a good outfielder?
Because he always catches flies.

What country always wins the trampoline event at the
    Olympics?
I don't know.
Czechoslovakia, because lots of Czechs bounce.

Golf must be a very dangerous game.
Why do you think that?
Yesterday's newspaper reported that a golfer shot 65 in the Open.

My car has a golf engine.
What's a golf engine?
One that goes putt, putt, putt.

In baseball why does it take longer to get from second base to third base than from first base to second base?

I don't know. Why?

Because there's a shortstop between second and third base.

Where are the largest diamonds in the world kept?
In baseball fields.

Did you hear the one about the bowler?
No, spare me.

My friend Juan was shot with a golf gun.
What's a golf gun?
I don't know, but it make a hole in Juan.

Does horseback riding give you a headache?
No, quite the reverse.

That baseball player was born in South America.
What part?
All of him.

I've been skiing since I was five years old.
Wow, you must be tired.

What is the best place to keep your baseball mitt?
In the glove compartment.

My father spends every day in court.
Is he a judge?
No, he plays tennis.

How many fish have you caught?
Well, if I catch this one I'm after and two more, I'll have
    three.

I hear your brother is a boxer.
That's right, he's Kid Candle.
Kid Candle?
One blow and he's out.

I hunted lions and tigers with a rifle.
I hunted lions and tigers with a bow and arrow.
I hunted lions and tigers with a club.
A club? Weren't you scared?
No, there were fifty people in the club.

What's the score?
35 to 0.
Aren't you discouraged by that score?
No, we haven't been to bat yet.

Did you hear about the person who took a ladder to the
  ball game because he wanted to shake hands with
  the Giants?

I've been eating beef all my life, and now I'm as strong
  as an ox.
That's funny. I've eaten fish all my life, and I can't swim
  a stroke.

Doctor, will I be able to play soccer after my leg is fixed?
Of course.
Great. I never could play soccer before.

How did the television set win the wrestling match?
It used its horizontal hold.

Don't worry. He hasn't laid a glove on you.
Then you better watch the referee—someone is
    beating me up.

What monster goes to baseball games?
A bat?
No, a double-header.

It's getting late and dark and we haven't hit anything
 yet.
Let's miss two more and then go home.

What do you call a girl's baseball glove?
A hermit.

Did you hear about the race driver at Indianapolis who
 had to make 50 pit stops?
Three for fuel, two to change tires, and forty-five to ask
 directions.

Why is a baseball stadium always cool?
Because it has a fan in every seat.

Is this a good lake for fish?
It must be—I can't get any of them to come out.

Did you hear the song about baseball?
No, why?
You should. It's really a big hit.

Why does a baseball player need a lot of gas?
It's a long drive to center field.

Do you know how to play baseball?
Certainly.
All right, tell me how to hold a bat.
That's easy—by the wings.

Why do baseball players make so much money?
Because a good batter always makes good dough.

My brother ran the 100-yard dash in six seconds.
That's impossible. The world record is nine seconds.
My brother knows a shortcut.

Did you hear about the person who won a letter in
 sports and asked a friend to read it to him?

(Baseball manager to player)
Remember all those batting and fielding tips I gave you
 to improve your game.
I sure do.
Well, forget them. We just traded you.

Name the four seasons.
Sure—football, basketball, baseball, and track.

What contains more feet in the winter than in
   the summer?
An ice skating rink.

Why did the man take a tree to the football game?
I don't know, why?
It wanted to root.

What do you dream about at night?
Baseball.
Don't you ever dream about anything else?
What? And miss my turn at bat?

This is a good spot for hunting.
How do you know?
The sign said: FINE FOR HUNTING.

If there are two flies in the kitchen, which one is the
    football player?
I don't know.
The one in the Sugar Bowl.

I don't guide hunters anymore—just fishermen.
Why?
I've never been mistaken for a fish.

I'm never going camping with a baseball player again.
Why?
I told him to pitch a tent and he threw it at me.

After the race the bicycle couldn't stand up.
Why not?
It was two-tired.

Did you hear about the person who took a rifle to the football game because the Lions and Bears were playing?

I can tell you the score of the game before it starts.
What is it?
Nothing to nothing.

What do you call a race track in space?
A star track.

I went riding today.
Horseback?
Sure. It got back two hours before I did.

Can you drive a golf ball?
No, it doesn't have a steering wheel.

You just got a hole in one on the tenth hole.
Great!
But we're playing on the sixth hole.

Why don't you play golf with Billy anymore?
Would you play with a cheat who writes down the
 wrong score and moves the ball when you're not
 looking?
Certainly not!
Well, neither will Billy.

What do you call a dog that plays baseball?
A catcher's mutt.

Interest your children in bowling. Get them off the streets and into the alleys.

How did you come to fall in?
I didn't come to fall in. I came to ice-skate.

Have you ever hunted bear?
No, but I've gone fishing in my bathing suit.

I'm going to the park to go jogging.
Good. Would you wear my self-winding watch. It needs
   the exercise.

Did you hear about the person who went to the football
   game because he thought a quarterback was a
   refund?

Why is tennis a noisy game?
Because each player raises a racket.

AH-CHOOOO

Have I done him any damage?
Not yet, but keep on swinging—the draft might give
  him a cold.

What do cheerleaders drink before every game?
Root beer.

Did you hear about the person who brought a rope to
  the ball game because he wanted to tie up the
  score?

What do they do with old bowling balls?
They give them to elephants to shoot marbles with.

Did you get hurt when you were on the football team?
No, only when the football team was on *me.*

What's the idea of hunting with last year's license?
I'm only shooting the ones I missed last year.

Do you want to see something really swell?
Sure.
Hit yourself on the head with a baseball bat.

FEB 1985